⊗RATED X-RAYS

BROOM-HILDA

by Russell Myers

tempo
books

GROSSET & DUNLAP
A FILMWAYS COMPANY
Publishers • New York

⊗RATED X-RAYS

RUSSELL MYERS

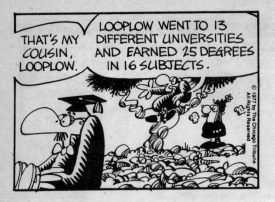

RUSSELL MYERS

RUSSELL MYERS

RUSSELL MYERS

RUSSELL MYERS

RUSSELL MYERS

RUSSELL MYERS

RUSSELL MYERS

RUSSELL MYERS

9-26

SLURP

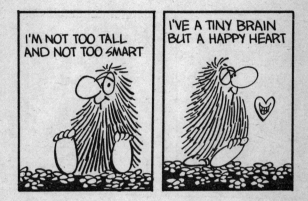

I FEEL I'M BRIGHT AND FULL OF WIT,

A CHARMING FOUR-EYED SOPHISTICATE.

A PRINCE WITHIN MY OWN DOMINION,

RUSSELL MYERS

I WISH OTHERS AGREED WITH MY OPINION.

10/12

THERE'S A SWELL OLD MONSTER MOVIE ON TV TONIGHT. C'MON OVER AND WATCH IT WITH ME!

10/24

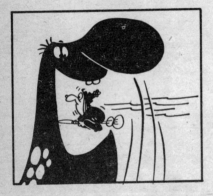

IRWIN, DO YOU BELIEVE IN CAPITAL PUNISHMENT?

I SURE DO!

GEE, I NEVER EXPECTED AN ANSWER LIKE THAT FROM _HIM_!

DON'T BE SO SURPRISED

HE THINKS CAPITAL PUNISHMENT MEANS SPANKING ALL THE POLITICIANS IN WASHINGTON, D.C.!